Department of Health

Seventh Report of the Committee for Monitoring Agreements on

Tobacco Advertising and Sponsorship

Chairman:
Sir John Blelloch, KCB

London: HMSO

© Crown copyright 1994

Applications for reproduction should be made to HMSO
First published 1994

ISBN 0 11 321818 4

Committee for Monitoring Agreements on Tobacco Advertising & Sponsorship

PO Box 3982, London SE1 8YJ

Chairman:	**Sir John Blelloch KCB**	**Your Reference:**
Joint Secretaries:	**Mrs G Silverman, Tel 071-630 9749**	**Our Reference:**
	Mr B Dyson, Tel 071-972 4220	**Date:** ₃ ᵃ June 1994

The Rt Hon Virginia Bottomley JP MP
Secretary of State for Health
Department of Health
Richmond House
79 Whitehall
London SW1A 2NS

Dear Secretary of State

I submit the Seventh Report of the Committee for Monitoring Agreements on Tobacco Advertising and Sponsorship. In submitting the Sixth Report I referred to the provision included in the new agreement reached in 1991 whereby the industry undertook to remove 50% of shop front advertising over a period of five years, and to the arrangements for auditing progress towards that objective. Part 6 of this Report summarises the results of the audit undertaken at the Committee's request and covering the year to July 1993. The audit shows that numbers of external permanent advertising signs for cigarettes and hand-rolling tobacco at retail premises have declined by at least 20% from the 1991 audit base for every category of sign and by geographic location, and by 83% in the case of signs visible from schools. Progress towards the original objective is therefore being maintained.

Last year I also referred to a query about whether, under the terms of the agreement to reduce permanent signs by 50%, a reduction in numbers could legitimately be accompanied by a compensating increase in the area of remaining tobacco advertisements. The industry had confirmed in response that, where permanent signs had been removed, they would not be replaced with similar non-permanent signs nor by material advertising other tobacco products. I reported that arrangements to monitor these further commitments would be included in the arrangements for the 1992/3 audit. Paragraphs 5-7 of Part 6 of this report pick up this point: the audit evidence confirms that the commitment has been honoured. The 1994 audit will include provisions to visit a further sample of sites where permanent window dressings have been removed as part of the reduction programme since it is to these that the concern about temporary material is particularly relevant. The outcome will be included in the next Report.

Following my 1993 submission, however, it was pointed out to me that what I had said did not deal fully with a further point of concern, namely that the impact of the required reductions might be lessened by removing a number of small signs advertising cigarettes or hand-rolling tobacco and replacing them with a single large display. The position on this point is that the removal of small items of non-permanent material does not count towards the required reductions in permanent material. Where small items of permanent material are removed, the scope for compensation is, in the Committee's view, in practice extremely limited, because the remaining permanent material is already likely to be as large as is practicable. What is more, because the reduction in permanent signs is being evenly applied by type of sign, the overall aggregate area of permanent advertising should reduce in proportion.

The Introduction to this Report sets out in paragraph 3 the main features of a further voluntary agreement reached between the Government and the Tobacco Industry, to be published shortly. When the details of this further agreement have been settled the Committee will of course need to consider if new monitoring arrangements are required. In the meantime, perhaps I could record the hope that, in settling the details, the opportunity is taken to resolve the question of how to interpret paragraph 4 of the Cigarette Promotion Code to which I drew attention in submitting the Fifth Report. The current text of the Code does not make clear whether or not companies may use advertisements in free papers and periodicals to invite adult smokers to apply for promotional vouchers. No complaint has been registered since then arising from this issue, but it is clearly better that the matter should be put beyond any doubt.

Parts 2 and 4 of this Report deal with the complaints handled by the Committee during the last year. There were fewer letters and queries than a year ago but the number of possible breaches contained in them was higher (40 as against 34) as well as the number of confirmed breaches (18 as against 6). Most of the complaints were against shop front advertising (28) and posters (6), and both of these are covered in the proposed new agreement. I welcome that. Most of the breaches were contained in one survey and related to door signs of an old design in which the health warnings had to be added in the form of a sticker. The company concerned had difficulties in ensuring that health warnings were always applied to, and remained fixed to, the signs. The company has discontinued the use of this type of sign. I welcome that too.

The average time taken to deal with complaints is, at twelve weeks, the same as a year ago. The Committee meets at roughly twelve weekly intervals and the majority of complaints are, quite properly, taken by it in Committee session rather than dealt with ex-Committee. Nevertheless it will continue to try to get the average down. Otherwise there are no other points in the Report that I need specifically to draw to your attention. As I have done, however, in each of my two previous Reports I would like to record again my thanks to the Committee for their approach to the conduct of business and to the resolution of tasks that have confronted them and to repeat what has been said in the past about the industry's continuing commitment to the letter and spirit of the Voluntary Agreements.

Yours sincerely

John Blelloch

JOHN BLELLOCH

Contents

SEVENTH REPORT OF THE COMMITTEE FOR
MONITORING AGREEMENTS ON TOBACCO
ADVERTISING AND SPONSORSHIP

1. Introduction

The Committee for Monitoring Agreements on Tobacco Advertising and
Sponsorship (COMATAS) was set up under the terms of the Voluntary Agreement
on Tobacco Products' Advertising and Promotion and Health Warnings, concluded
on 1 April 1986 between HM Government and the United Kingdom tobacco industry
as represented by the Tobacco Advisory Council, now the Tobacco Manufacturers
Association (TMA), and the Imported Tobacco Products Advisory Council (ITPAC).

2.   A new agreement on advertising and promotion was published on 9 September
1991 and revised on 1 January 1992 to reflect the requirements of the EC Directive
on tobacco products labelling. The agreement was replaced in November 1992 by
a new agreement in identical terms, save for an additional clause designed to ensure
compliance with the Restrictive Trade Practices Act 1976.

3.   The Government and the Industry have recently agreed a new package of
measures on advertising and promotion, which will form the basis for a revised
voluntary agreement to be published shortly.   The main features of the new
agreement will be:

Outdoor advertising

- the removal of all permanent shopfront advertising for all tobacco products by
  the end of 1996;

- a reduction in the expenditure allowed on cigarette poster advertising by 40 per
  cent;

- the removal of all small poster advertising for cigarettes and hand-rolling
  tobacco, including bus stop advertising (48 sheet posters and above will still be
  allowed);

- the removal of all mobile advertising for cigarettes and hand-rolling tobacco;

- the removal of all poster advertising for all tobacco products from within a 200
  metre radius of school entrances.

<u>Health warnings</u>

- an increase in the size of the health warnings on cigarette and hand-rolling tobacco advertisements to 20 per cent of the total area, and an increase in the size of the lettering of the warning by approximately 80 per cent in posters and 50 per cent in press advertisements. The presentation of the health warnings will be rotated between black lettering on a white background and white lettering on a black background;

- the introduction of health warnings on cigar and pipe tobacco advertisements, covering 10 per cent of the total area;

- a requirement for all point of sale advertising material for all tobacco products to carry health warnings (not just larger items of cigarette and hand-rolling tobacco advertising) and the introduction of health warnings on certain items of promotional material for cigarettes and hand-rolling tobacco;

<u>Other main provisions</u>

- the controls on the content of cigarette advertisements, operated by the Advertising Standards Authority, will prevent the use of humour in cigarette advertisements which would be likely to have a particular appeal to the young;

- the introduction of a new Code of Practice to help ensure that free samples of cigarettes are not available to under 18s;

- a ban on advertising for tobacco products on computer games or on other computer software;

- a provision for increased expenditure by COMATAS on monitoring compliance with the new agreement.

Terms of Reference

4. The Committee's task is to monitor the operation of the Voluntary Agreement on Advertising and Promotion, and the Voluntary Agreement on Sponsorship of Sport by Tobacco Companies in the UK concluded in January 1987. Summaries of the main provisions of these Agreements are to be found in Annexes A and B. The Committee will monitor the new agreement on advertising and promotion when it comes into force.

5. The Committee's terms of reference are set out in Appendix 7 to the Voluntary Agreement on Advertising and Promotion and are as follows:

"a. To keep under review all matters relating to the operation of the voluntary agreement other than those relating directly to the operation of the Cigarette Advertising Code and monitored by the Advertising Standards Authority, or matters which are the responsibility of the BBC or ITC.

2

b. To ensure that the terms of the voluntary agreement are properly observed and are interpreted with consistency.

c. To receive full details of all complaints sent by the public or public bodies to the Government Departments concerned, and of the responses by those companies to whom the complaints were referred. In the case of disputed matters or those which raise general issues relevant to the observance of the agreement, to take a view and, where appropriate, communicate that view to the parties concerned.

d. To report annually to Ministers, and to member companies through the TAC [now the TMA] and ITPAC respectively, on the general implementation of the agreement".

Method of Working

6. The Committee is required to meet as often as business demands and at least quarterly. Its first meeting was in December 1986 and it has so far met a total of thirty-five times, four since the publication of the Sixth Annual Report in June 1993. In keeping with the rules set out in the Agreement on Advertising and Promotion its proceedings are confidential except that its annual report may be published at the discretion of Ministers following consultation with the tobacco industry. After consultation with the tobacco industry, and with the complete agreement of the Committee, the six previous annual reports have been published. The Committee is serviced by a joint secretariat provided by the Government and the Tobacco Manufacturers Association.

7. The Committee arranges for the investigation of complaints submitted by the public. In most cases the relevant company is asked to carry out an investigation and report back to the Committee, although in some cases the Secretariat investigates. The Committee then takes a view. The Committee decided at an early stage that to rely solely on the random incidence of complaints as a measure of compliance by the industry would not be sufficient in view of the volume and intensity of advertising material in use. Accordingly, in order to provide a more systematic basis for evaluation and in line with its remit, the Committee commissions independent consultants to investigate how certain aspects of the agreements are being adhered to. The Committee has so far commissioned nine studies:

3

i.   health warnings on shop-front advertising (two studies);

ii.   the location of cigarette and hand-rolling tobacco brand advertising on posters in relation to schools;

iii.   general aspects of two televised sporting events sponsored by tobacco companies;

iv.   adherence to the Cigarette Promotion Code (which forms part of the voluntary agreement) with specific reference to direct mail;

v.   audit of permanent shopfront advertising to establish the base figure for 1 July 1991 from which the 50 per cent reduction over 5 years would take place, as detailed in the 1991 Agreement;

vi.   audits of the first and second years of progress towards the 50 per cent reduction in permanent shopfront advertising;

vii.   a survey to assess whether the industry had met its undertaking not to replace permanent shopfront advertising material for cigarettes and hand-rolling tobacco with permanent advertising material for other tobacco products or with similar non-permanent signs for any tobacco products.

The results of the first four studies were presented in the first two Annual Reports. The study of direct mail procedures was reported in the Fourth and Fifth Annual Reports. The Sixth Report included a report of the baseline audit of permanent shopfront advertising and the first audit of progress towards the 50 per cent reduction. Chapter 6 of this Report summarises the results of the two most recent studies.

Membership   8.   The Committee is composed of equal numbers of representatives of the Government departments concerned and the tobacco industry, under an independent Chairman appointed with the agreement of Ministers and the Chairman of the Tobacco Manufacturers Association. The current Chairman, Sir John Blelloch KCB, was appointed in April 1991. As at 1 June 1994 the Committee members were:

Sir John Blelloch KCB Chairman

Mr T S Heppell CB (DoH)	Mr D Swan (TMA)
Mr G Podger (DoH)	Mr D R Hare (TMA)
Ms L Lockyer (DoH)	Mr I E Birks (Gallaher Ltd)
Mr E Miller (Scottish Office)	Mr E D Oxberry (Rothmans (UK) Ltd)
Mr D Adams (Welsh Office)	Mr P L C Middleton (Imperial Tobacco Ltd)
Mr D Baker (DHSS NI)	Mr K Jewsbury (R J Reynolds)
Miss A Stewart (DNH)	Mr R Loader (ITPAC)

Joint Secretaries

Mr B Dyson (DoH)   Mrs G Silverman (TMA)

9. The Committee thanks Norman Hale and Craig Muir of the Department of Health and Alan King of the Scottish Office who left the Committee during the year and the previous Secretaries Marguerite Weatherseed (DoH) and Pauline Elcome (TMA).

Finances

10. The Committee is funded jointly by the Government and the Industry. In the period 1 February 1993 to 31 January 1994 committed expenditure (including VAT) was as follows:

Permanent Shopfront Audit	£41,581.62
Survey of Replacement of Permanent Signage	£11,733.55
Chairman's fees	£2,000.00

Members' and Secretaries' expenses were met by their Department or Company.

2 Analysis of Responses to Complaints on Tobacco Advertising

1. The Sixth Annual Report recorded one complaint outstanding on tobacco advertising. The Committee found that this had been an inadvertent breach of the agreement.

Sources of Complaints

2. During its seventh year the Committee received eight letters of complaint and two queries on tobacco advertising. Seven letters of complaints and one query were from private individuals. The other letter of complaint came from a local authority and the other query from a health organisation.

Nature of Complaints

3. The letters of complaint gave details of 36 items which were thought to be possible breaches of the voluntary agreement on advertising and promotion. The majority of these arose from a single study of health warnings on shopfront and point-of-sale advertising material. The remaining items included six poster advertisements close to schools, which were thought to be in breach of paragraph 1.8 of the agreement.

Table 2.1 *Complaints: advertising medium*

Shops	28
Posters	6
Press	1
Promotions	1
TOTAL	36

Committee Conclusions

4.   The Committee concluded that 17 items had been in breach of the agreement. Six of these were held to be inadvertent breaches, for instance where a health warning had been obscured or removed by the actions of a third party for whom the tobacco company could not be held responsible. Thus the item was technically in breach of the agreement, but the tobacco industry was not to blame. All but one of the other eleven breaches were items of shopfront advertising material without health warnings. In most cases, these were door signs which were designed to have the health warning added in the form of a sticker. The company discontinued this type of sign because of difficulties in ensuring that health warnings were always applied to, and remained fixed to, the signs.

5.   In 13 cases, there had been no breach. In a further five cases, the Committee was unable to reach a conclusion, because there was insufficient information about the alleged breach. One item was outside the scope of the voluntary agreement.

Table 2.2   *Committee Conclusions*

Items in breach	17 (6 inadvertent)
Items not in breach	13
Insufficient evidence to reach a conclusion	5
Items outside the scope of the agreement	1
TOTAL	36

Time taken to respond to complaints

6.   The Secretariat instigate immediate investigations of all complaints received by the Committee, except where they clearly fall outside the scope of the agreement. However, it is not always possible to send a final reply to the complainant until after the Committee has reached a view on the complaint at one of its quarterly meetings. Since the Sixth Annual Report was published, the average time taken to deal with complaints and queries (including those about sports sponsorship) has been 12 weeks.

3 Restrictions on Advertising in Young Women's Magazines

1. The voluntary agreement on advertising and promotion provides that advertisements for cigarettes or hand-rolling tobacco will not be placed in magazines for which the female readership aged 15-24 is 25 per cent or more of the total adult readership (aged 15 and over.)

2. The following table lists those magazines which, on the basis of average readership figures for the four quarters ending December 1993, should not carry cigarette or hand-rolling tobacco advertising. Any newly published magazine or periodical may not carry such advertising until the readership figures for the first six months have been established.

Table 2.3 *Young Women's Magazines: 1994 Proscribed Publications List*

Publications whose female readership aged 15-24 exceeds
25% of total adult readers (aged 15 and above)

Title	% Female readership aged 15-24
Looks	79
Catch	77
Mizz	77
More!	73
'19'	68
My Guy	62
Just Seventeen	59
Big!	52
Company	44
Clothes Show Magazine	43
Smash Hits	38
The Face	35
Elle	34
Hair Flair	33
Marie Claire	33
Top Santé	32
Flicks	31
Wedding and Home	30
Hair	29
New Woman	29
Cosmopolitan	28
Elle Decoration	26
Select	26
Brides & Setting Up Home	25
Raw	25

NRS Readership Survey, January - December 1993

4 Sports Sponsorship

1.   The current voluntary agreement on sports sponsorship came into force in January 1987. Its main provisions are set out in Annex B.

2.   In the last year, the Committee received four complaints in respect of sports sponsorship. The Committee found that one complaint was outside the scope of the agreement and reserved its position on one complaint. Of the other complaints, one alleged a breach of the requirement to place a health warning on static promotional signs likely to come within television coverage at sponsored sporting events. The Committee found that no breach had occurred in this case. The other complaint concerned the display of a cigarette brand symbol on participants and their equipment in a sporting activity televised in the UK. The Committee concluded that this had been in breach of the agreement.

3.   As in previous years, each tobacco company fulfilled the undertaking in the voluntary agreement to notify the Department of National Heritage of its sponsorship plans for the year ahead and any subsequent changes to those plans.

5 Financial Aspects of the Agreements

Advertising expenditure

1. The agreements require the Tobacco Manufacturers Association and the Imported Tobacco Products Advisory Council to supply the Government in confidence with annual figures on industry expenditure on press and poster advertising and on sports sponsorship.

2. As in previous years, the figures supplied by the Tobacco Manufacturers Association for the year ending 31 March 1993 were certified by an auditor. Each company sent its figures, accompanied by a certificate from its auditors, to the Tobacco Manufacturers Association. These figures were aggregated, and the Tobacco Manufacturers Association's auditors then certified that the aggregate figure was an accurate sum of the figures from the individual companies. The aggregated figures were then sent to the Department of Health or (in the case of sports sponsorship) the Department of National Heritage, accompanied by the auditor's certificate.

Limit on spending on cigarette brand poster advertising

3. The agreement on advertising and promotion says (in paragraphs 1.3 and 1.4, page 3):

"The companies represented by the Tobacco Manufacturers Association will continue to limit their expenditure on cigarette brand poster advertising in each successive twelve month period from 1 April 1991 to 50% in aggregate of the level in the year ending 31 March 1980, subject to allowances for inflation as agreed with the DH.

"The companies represented by the Imported Tobacco Products Advisory Council will ensure that the expenditure on poster advertising of cigarette brands that they import does not exceed 3.5% in aggregate of the limit accepted by the Tobacco Manufacturers Association for the twelve month period ending 31 March in each year of the agreement."

4. The figures from the Tobacco Manufacturers Association (certified by the auditors) for cigarette brand poster advertising in 1992/93, show that expenditure was within the total permitted spend after making allowances for inflation. The Department of Health has informed the Committee that on the basis of the figures supplied by the Imported Tobacco Products Advisory Council, the amount spent by their members on cigarette brand poster advertising was within the agreed expenditure limit.

Limit on spending on sports sponsorship

5. The agreement on Sports Sponsorship provides for limits for the amount to be spent on the sponsorship of sport in the UK by each individual company in any financial year except after prior consultation with the Minister. The aggregated data provided by the Tobacco Manufacturers Association, and certified by audit, show that expenditure on sports sponsorship for the year 1992/93 was within the allowed spend using 1985 as a base year and that the proportion of total expenditure spent on media advertising and other promotional material directly related to the events, otherwise than at events, was less than 20 per cent.

6 Independent Investigations Commissioned by the Committee

Audit of Permanent Shopfront Material

1. As part of the revised agreement on advertising and promotion which first came into force in September 1991, the industry undertook to reduce the total number of advertising signs for cigarette and hand-rolling tobacco brands at retail premises by 50 per cent over five years. The agreement requires the industry to take all reasonable steps to ensure that the reduction is applied evenly over time, by type of sign and by geographic location. Priority should be given to reducing the number of permanent signs on shops clearly visible from schools.

2. Coopers and Lybrand were appointed to carry out an annual independent audit to monitor progress in this undertaking. The audit for the year from July 1991 (reported in the Sixth Annual Report) indicated that permanent shopfront advertising for cigarettes and hand-rolling tobacco had declined by at least 10 per cent for every category of sign and by geographic location. The percentage of signs visible from schools had decreased by 68 per cent.

3. In 1993 Coopers and Lybrand undertook a further audit to validate progress towards the targets. The auditors again reviewed the companies' systems for collecting, holding, and amending their records of permanent signs. From these records the companies provided the auditors with information about the reduction made in the year from July 1992. The auditors tested the accuracy of this information by a sample of visits to 350 retail outlets, extending the sample by 100 from the previous year.

4. The 1993 audit indicated that external permanent advertising signs for cigarettes and hand-rolling tobacco at retail premises had declined by at least 20 per cent from the 1991 audit base for every category of sign and by geographic location. The number of signs visible from schools had fallen by 83 per cent from the audit base. The auditors declared these figures as representing fairly, in all material respects, the situation of external permanent cigarette and hand-rolling tobacco advertising signs at retail premises in July 1993 and the decrease from the 1991 audit base.

Survey of replacement

of permanent signage

5. The industry made a further commitment in 1992 not to replace:

i.   external permanent advertising signs with similar non-permanent signs for any tobacco products;

ii. such permanent cigarette shopfront advertising material with permanent advertising for other tobacco products.

6. Coopers and Lybrand carried out a survey to ensure that the industry had met this undertaking. The auditors selected a sample of 100 sites from which permanent advertising had been removed.   They visited these sites to check whether permanent material had been replaced with similar non-permanent material or with permanent advertisements for cigars or pipe tobacco. For the purposes of the survey, similarity between permanent and non-permanent material was defined in terms of its impact, its extent or coverage, and the materials used.

7. There was no evidence from the auditors' survey that external permanent advertising signs for cigarettes or hand-rolling tobacco had been replaced with similar non-permanent signs or with advertising for other tobacco products.

MAIN PROVISIONS OF THE AGREEMENT ON TOBACCO PRODUCTS' ADVERTISING AND PROMOTION FIRST PUBLISHED IN SEPTEMBER 1991, REVISED JANUARY 1992, AND RE-MADE IN NOVEMBER 1992

1. General

The companies will:

- limit their annual expenditure on cigarette brand poster advertising to 50% of that spent in 1980 in real terms;

- discontinue advertising of cigarette or hand-rolling tobacco brands on the exterior of vehicles, other than public service vehicles, trams, trolley buses, taxis, and vehicles owned by or contracted to the companies;

- endeavour to ensure that other goods bearing tobacco brand names or designs, in a manner having the effect of associating those goods with tobacco products, are not produced for, sold or given away to persons under 18;

- continue to ensure that promotional offers are confined to adult smokers and that there are no deliveries of unaddressed or anonymously addressed offers;

- maintain their agreement not to advertise cigarettes or hand-rolling tobacco at cinemas, in video cassettes for sale or hire to the public, or on airships, on balloons or from banner-towing aeroplanes.

2. Schools

There will be no static outdoor cigarette and hand-rolling tobacco brand advertising (excluding signs on retail premises) in close proximity to, and clearly visible and identifiable from within buildings or boundaries of:

- schools or places of education for young people;

- playgrounds predominantly used by young people under 18 years of age, associated with a school or place of education, or provided by local authorities specifically for use by children and containing play items, for example, swings, climbing frames, slides, etc.

Nor will any such advertising be placed adjacent to entrances and exits, or the pavements forming the boundaries to such schools, places of education and playgrounds.

3. Reduction in Shopfront Advertising

The industry undertakes to reduce the total number of external permanent advertising signs for cigarettes and hand-rolling tobacco at retail premises by 50% over five years. The reductions will be validated annually by independent audit with reference to the records held by each company. The results of the audit will be made available to COMATAS.

The industry will take all reasonable steps to ensure that the reduction is applied evenly over time, by type of sign and by geographic location.

Priority will be given to reducing the number of permanent signs on shops clearly visible from schools.

4. Young Women's Magazines

No advertising of cigarette or hand-rolling tobacco brands will be placed in magazines or periodicals published in their own right when it is apparent at the time the advertisement is placed that the readership amongst young women aged 15-24 is 25% or more of the total adult readership. For established magazines, the average of the previous four quarterly reports of the National Readership Survey will be the basis on which a decision is taken. No advertising of cigarette or hand-rolling brands will be placed in a newly published magazine or periodical published in its own right until the readership figures for the first six months have been published.

5. Health Warnings

The companies will comply with the Government's request that they should print the warnings which are required by law to appear on the back face of a cigarette packet in related advertising. They will also comply with the Government's request that they should print the warnings required by law to appear on the side opposite to the most visible surface of hand-rolling tobacco packets in related advertising. The companies will employ the relevant warnings in rotation. The space in press and poster advertising devoted to the health warning and, where relevant, the tar and nicotine yield statements will be 17.5% of the area of the advertisement.

The health warning and, where relevant, the tar and nicotine yield statements will be incorporated in cigarette or hand-rolling tobacco brand advertising material of 40 sq ins or more, supplied by the companies for display at retail sales points.

All temporary and all new, permanent advertising material for cigarettes or hand-rolling tobacco supplied to retailers will carry the appropriate health warning. All existing permanent shopfront advertising for cigarettes or hand-rolling tobacco, issued to retailers by the industry, should carry health warnings by the end of June 1991. Thereafter the industry will place health warnings on any such signs which it has been unable to trace, but which have been brought to its attention by a third party through the COMATAS Secretariat. All material which carried the health warning prescribed by the 1983 voluntary agreement will carry the warning prescribed by this agreement as material is normally replaced or refurbished.

MAIN PROVISIONS OF THE AGREEMENT ON SPONSORSHIP OF SPORT BY TOBACCO COMPANIES (AGREED IN JANUARY 1987)

1.   The agreement sets out more specific controls on tobacco companies' involvement in sponsoring sporting activities, particularly televised sport. Companies will not sponsor sporting activities which appeal mainly to spectators under 18.

Expenditure

2.   Overall annual expenditure on sponsorship is reduced to 1985 levels in real terms and a ceiling of 20% is placed on advertising and promotional activity. Aggregated annual expenditure returns will be submitted to the department responsible (now the Department of National Heritage), who may publish the data.

Health Warnings

3.   The agreement provides for the wider use of health warnings. They must, as far as possible, be consistent with those applicable to cigarette advertisements. The size of health warnings at televised events is increased from 10% of the total area of the sign to 15%.

Television

4.   Television companies have their own codes of practice which, of course, they will continue to apply. Appendix 1 to the agreement sets out revised controls on static signs at televised sporting activities.

Media Advertising

5.   Under the agreement, media advertising must be designed as far as possible not to conflict with the letter and spirit of the Cigarette Code in the British Code of Advertising Practice. Advertisements shall not include any representation of a cigarette or a cigarette pack and shall not depict participants in a sport or their equipment.

Printed in the United Kingdom for HMSO
Dd 299755 7/94 C5 3396 17434